Third Position Study Book for the Violin

book one

by Cassia Harvey

CHP217

©2013 by C. Harvey Publications All Rights Reserved.

www.charveypublications.com - print books
www.learnstrings.com - PDF downloadable books
www.harveystringarrangements.com - chamber music

Third Position Study Book for the Violin, Book One

1

Cassia Harvey

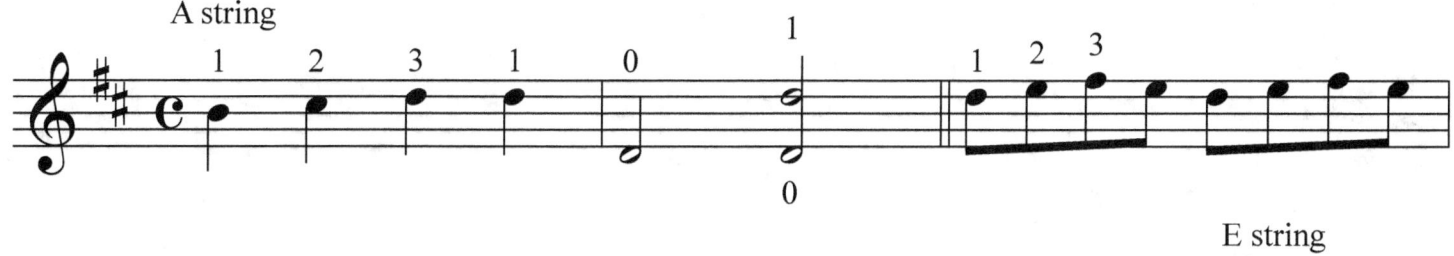

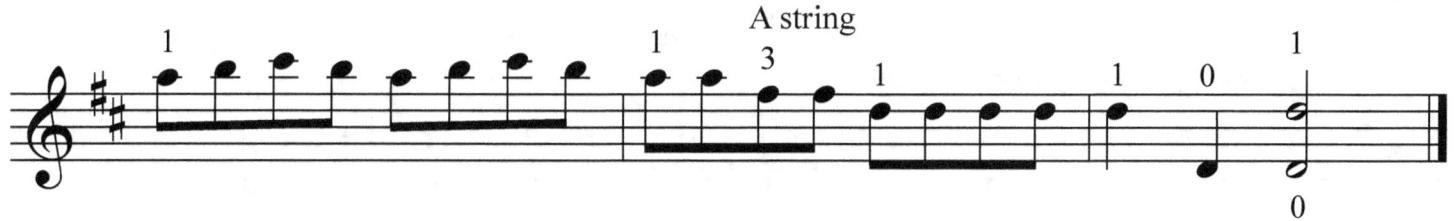

The Grey Goose: A Folk Song

©2013 C. Harvey Publications All Rights Reserved.

2

Walking with the Wagons

Third Position Study Book for the Violin, Book One

3

Along the River

4

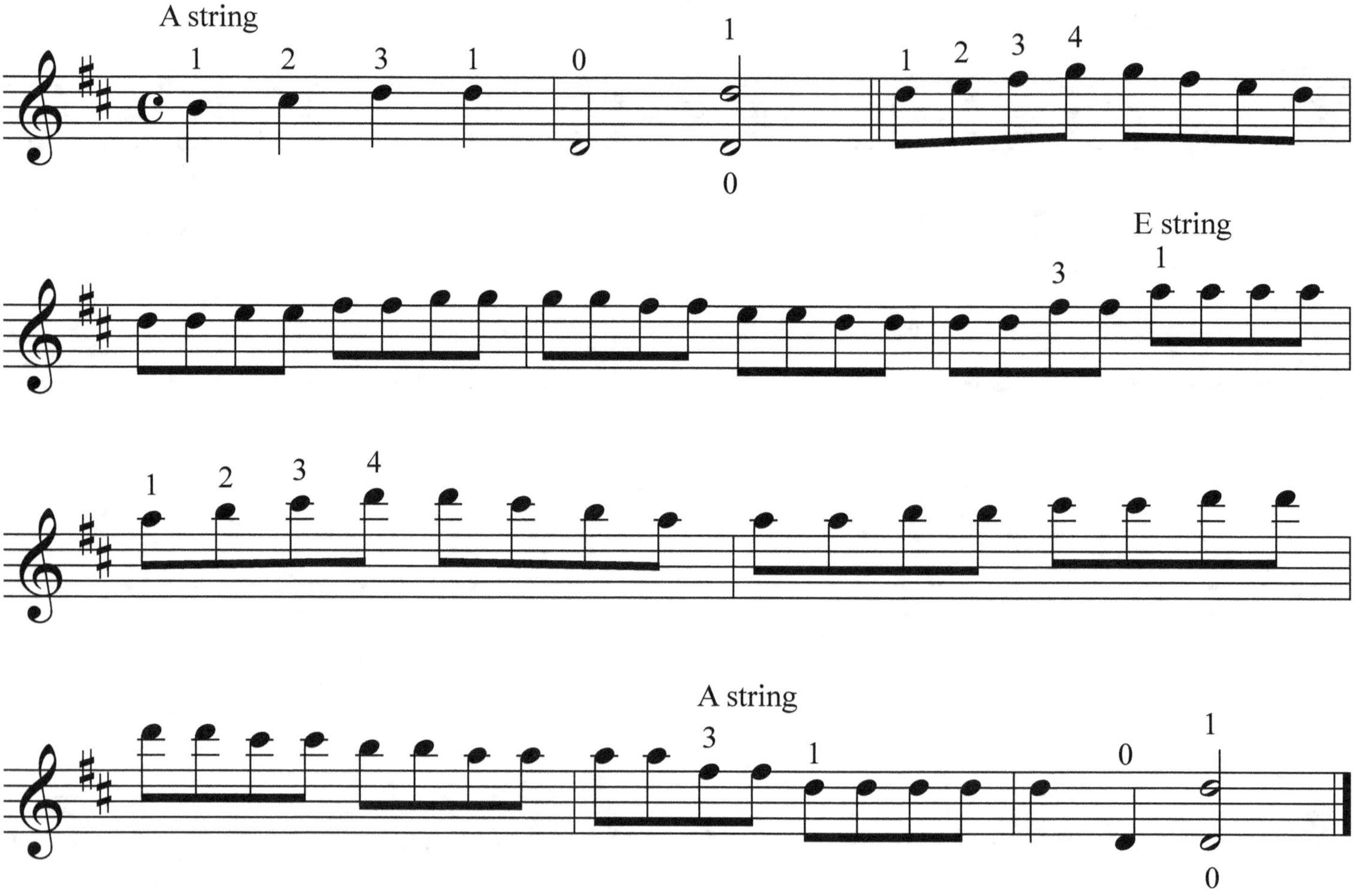

French Dance: A Folk Tune

5

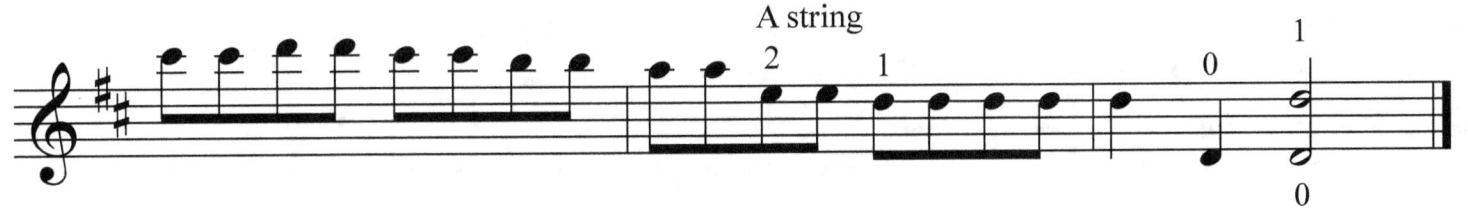

The Southerly Wind: A Folk Round

6

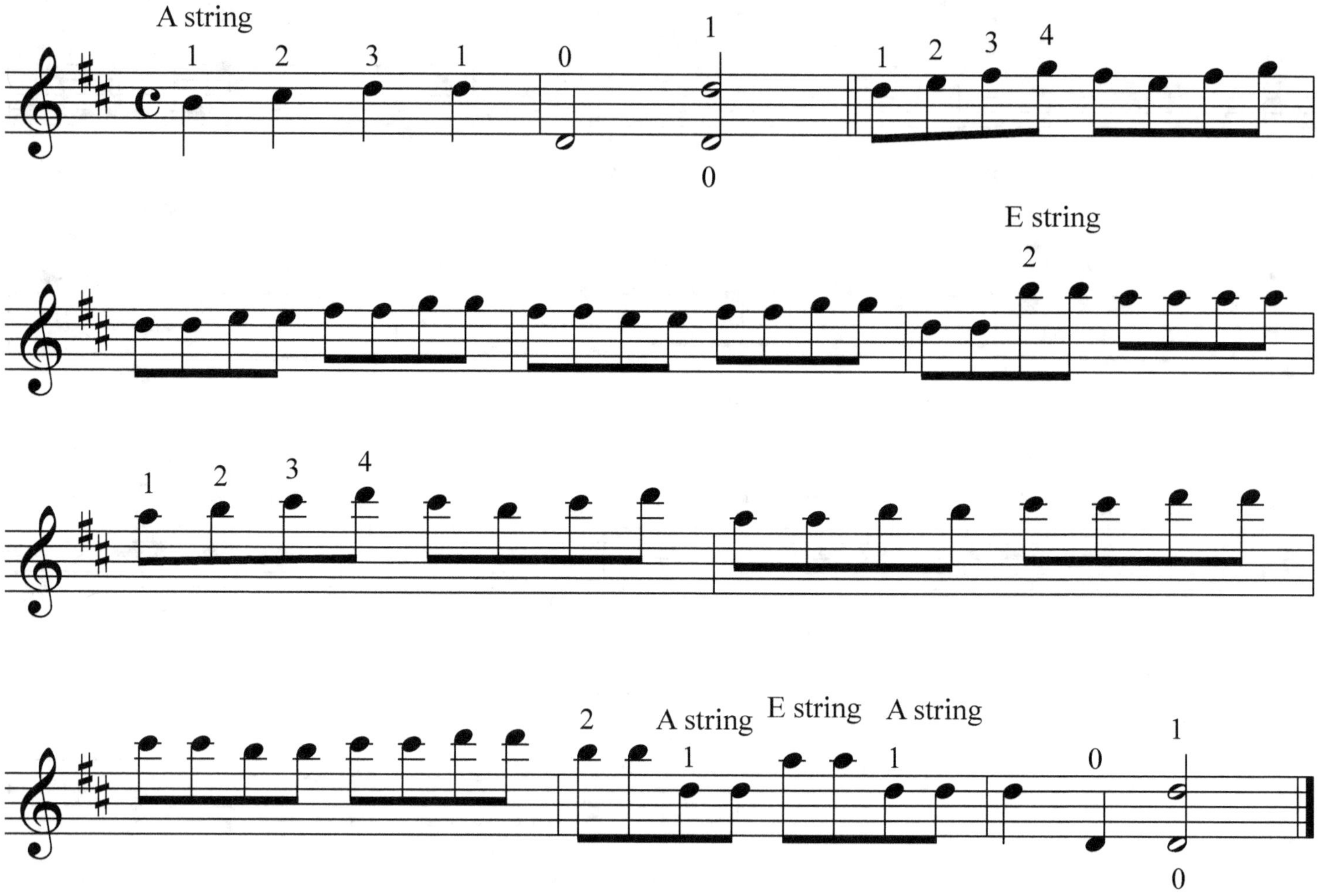

Bayly's Gaily the Troubadour

Third Position Study Book for the Violin, Book One

7

Reuben and Rachel: A Folk Song

8

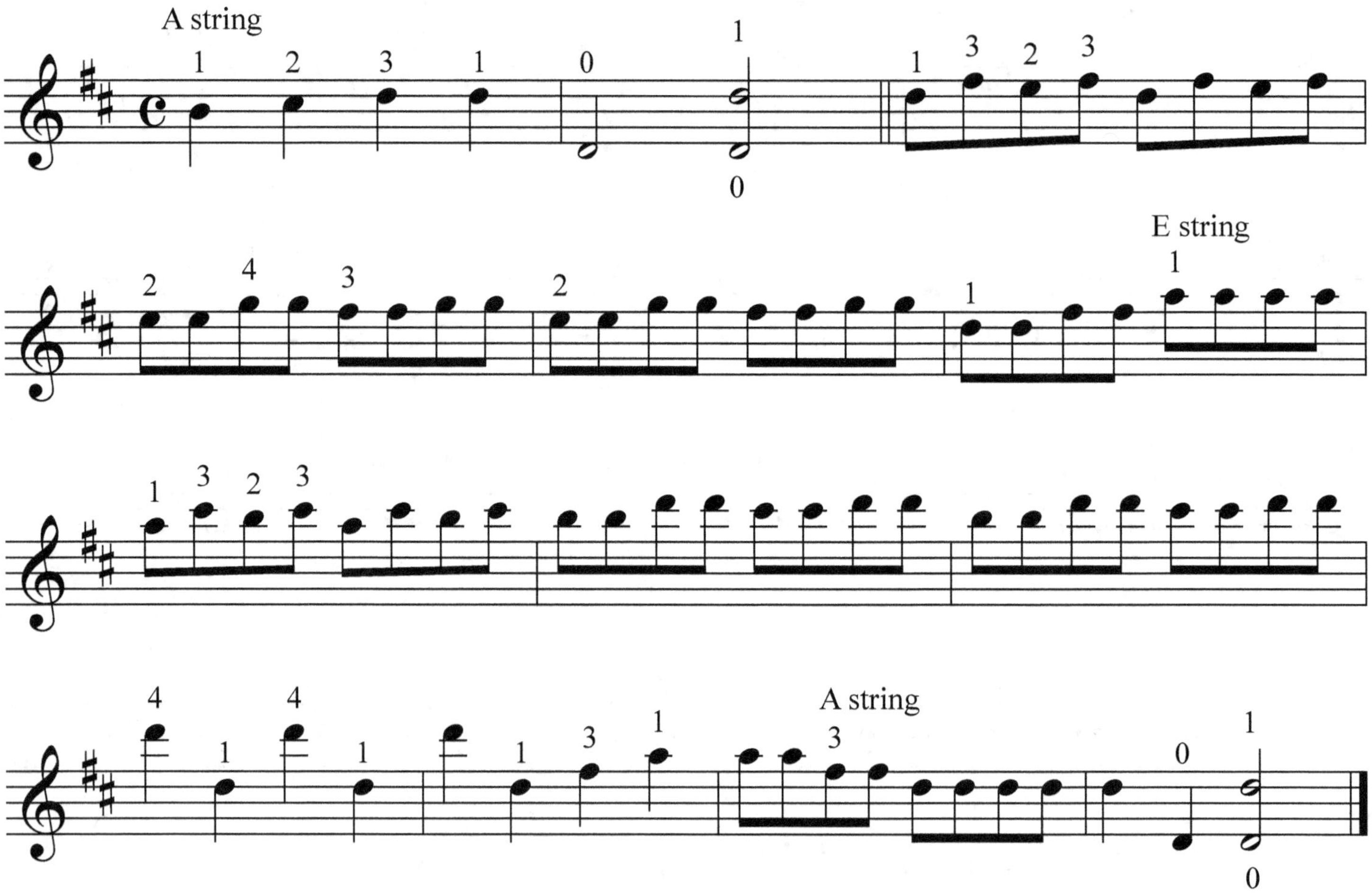

Leezie Lindsay: A Folk Song

Third Position Study Book for the Violin, Book One

9

Scotland's Burning: A Round

11

Chicago Street Song: A Folk Tune

12

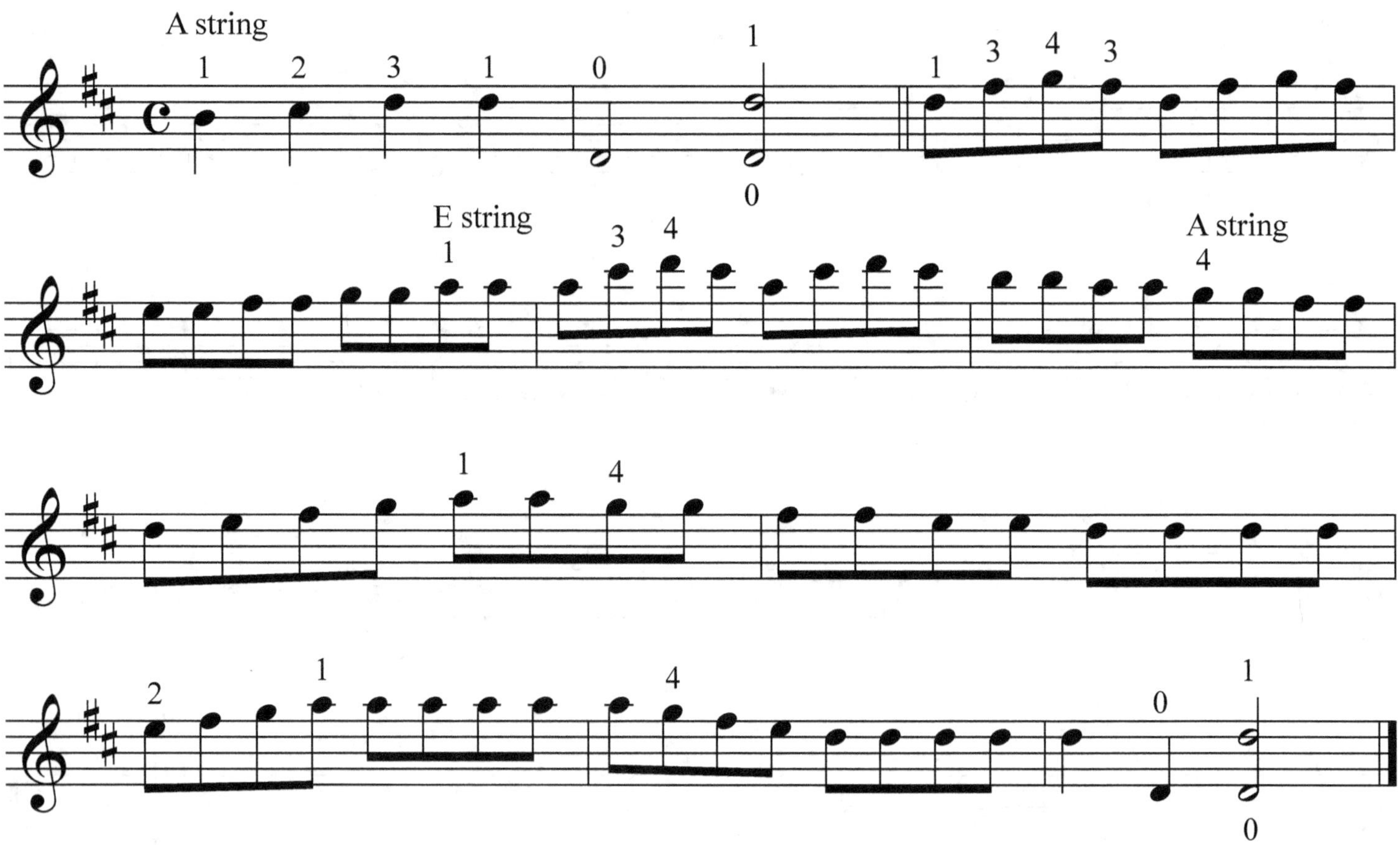

Mozart's Theme

13

The Tree in the Wood: A Folk Song

14

Row, Row, Row Your Boat: A Folk Round

15

Mozart's Alphabet Song

16

Believe Me, if All Those Endearing Young Charms: A Folk Tune

17

French-Canadian Folk Song

18

Peasant Dance

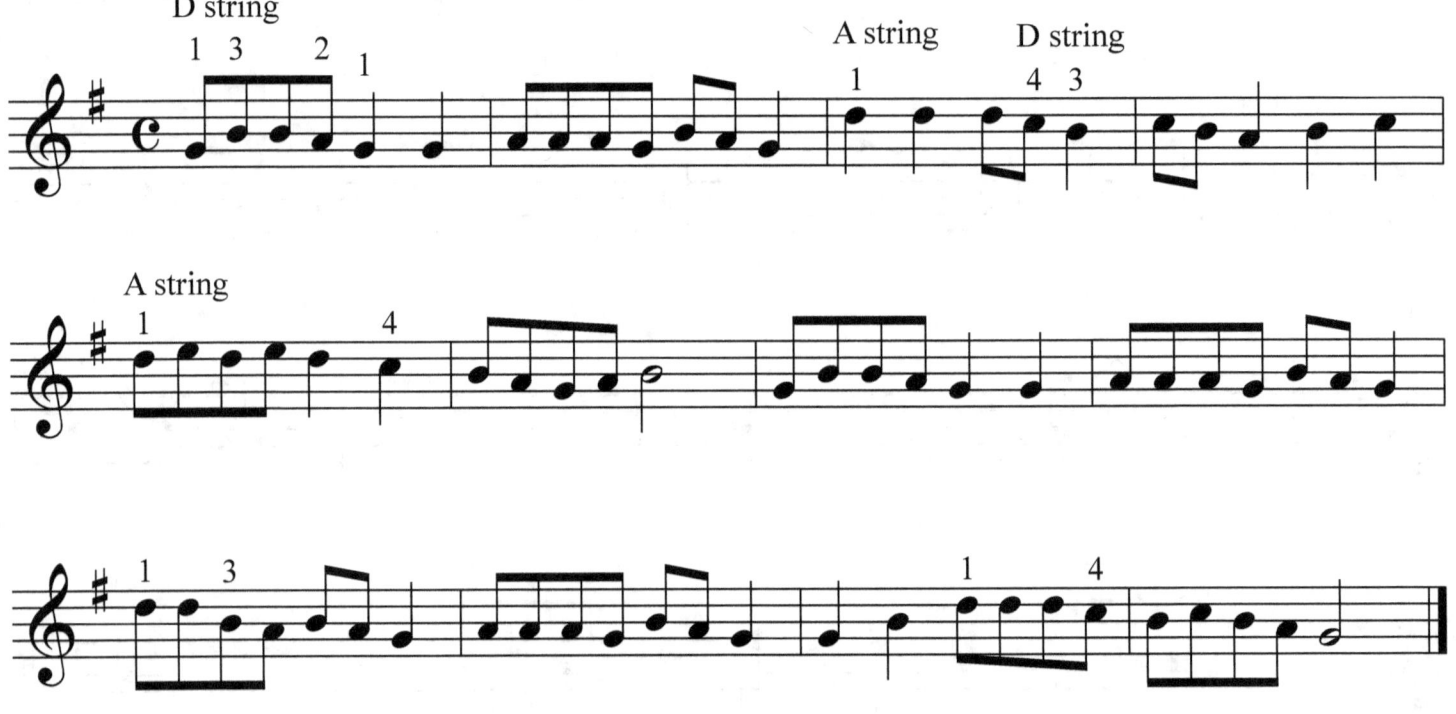

19

Sleep Baby Sleep; A Traditional Lullaby

20

May Dance: A Folk Tune

21

Beethoven's German Dance

22

Jasmine Flower: A Folk Melody

23

D string

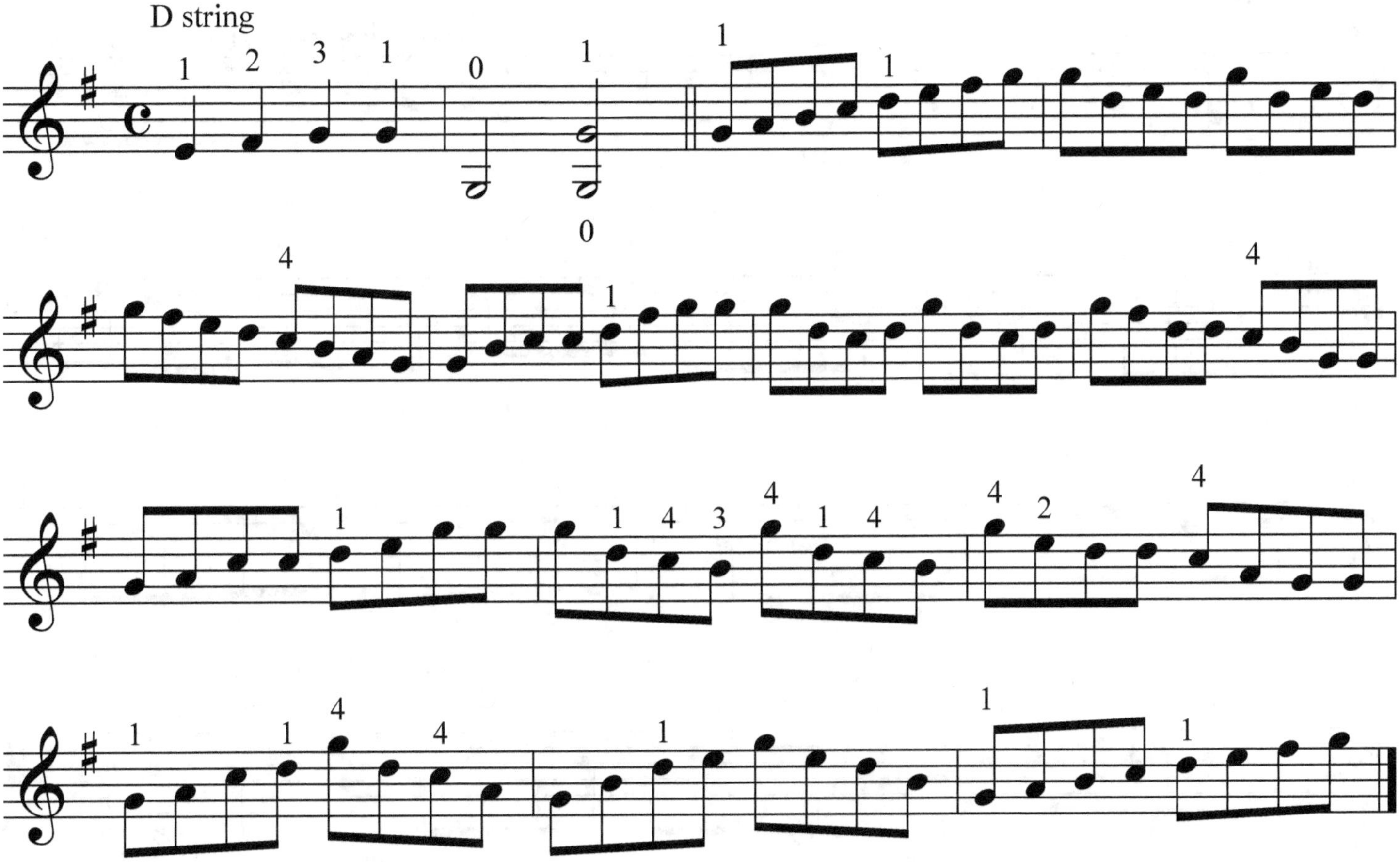

The Woman and the Peddler: A Folk Tune

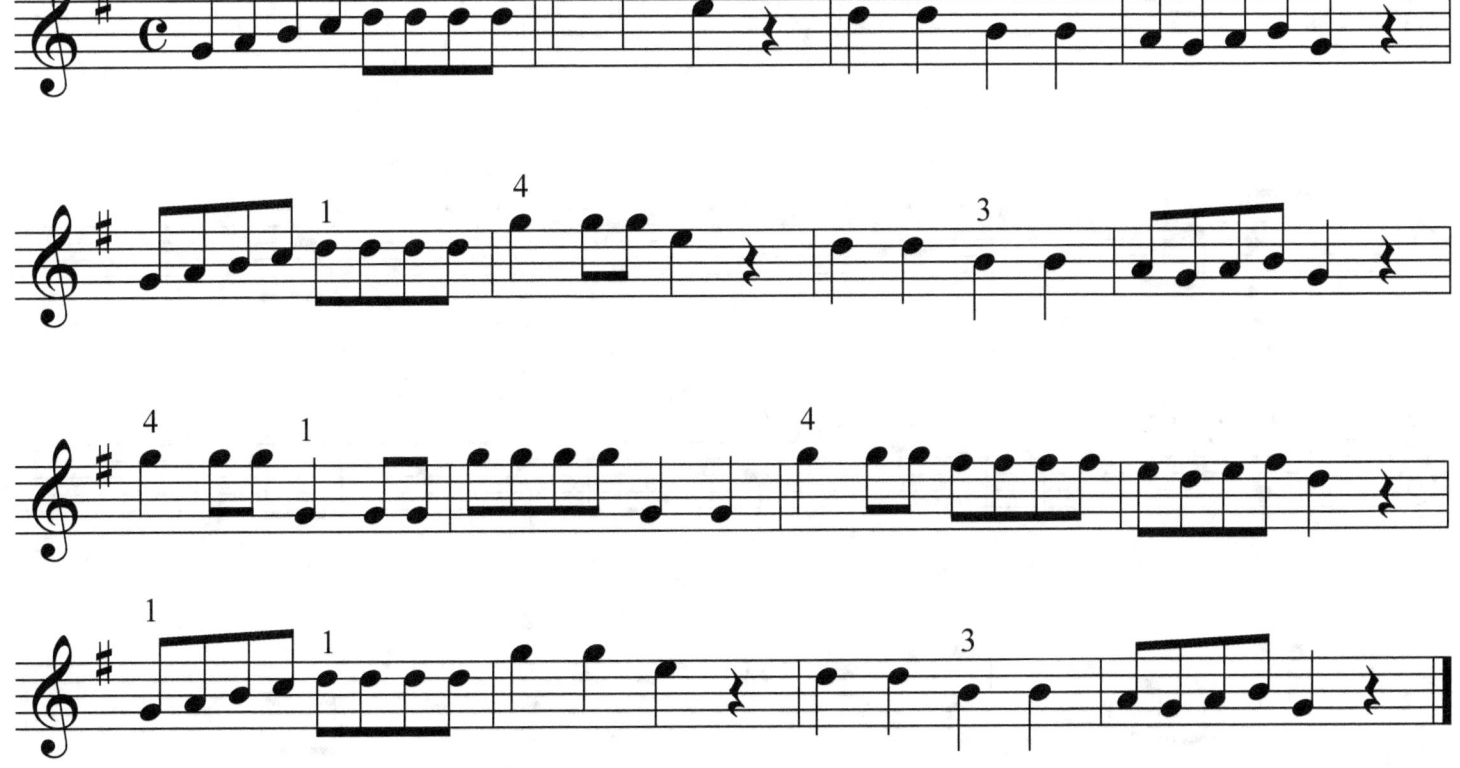

24

Ganne's La Czarine

Third Position Study Book for the Violin, Book One

25

Bach's Minuet

26

Masque

Praetorious' Dance

28

Aiken Drum: A Folk Tune

29

Giroflé, Girofla: A Folk Song

30

Behr's Dance

Lavender's Blue: A Folk Song

32

Couperin's Les Moissonneurs

You Might Also Like:

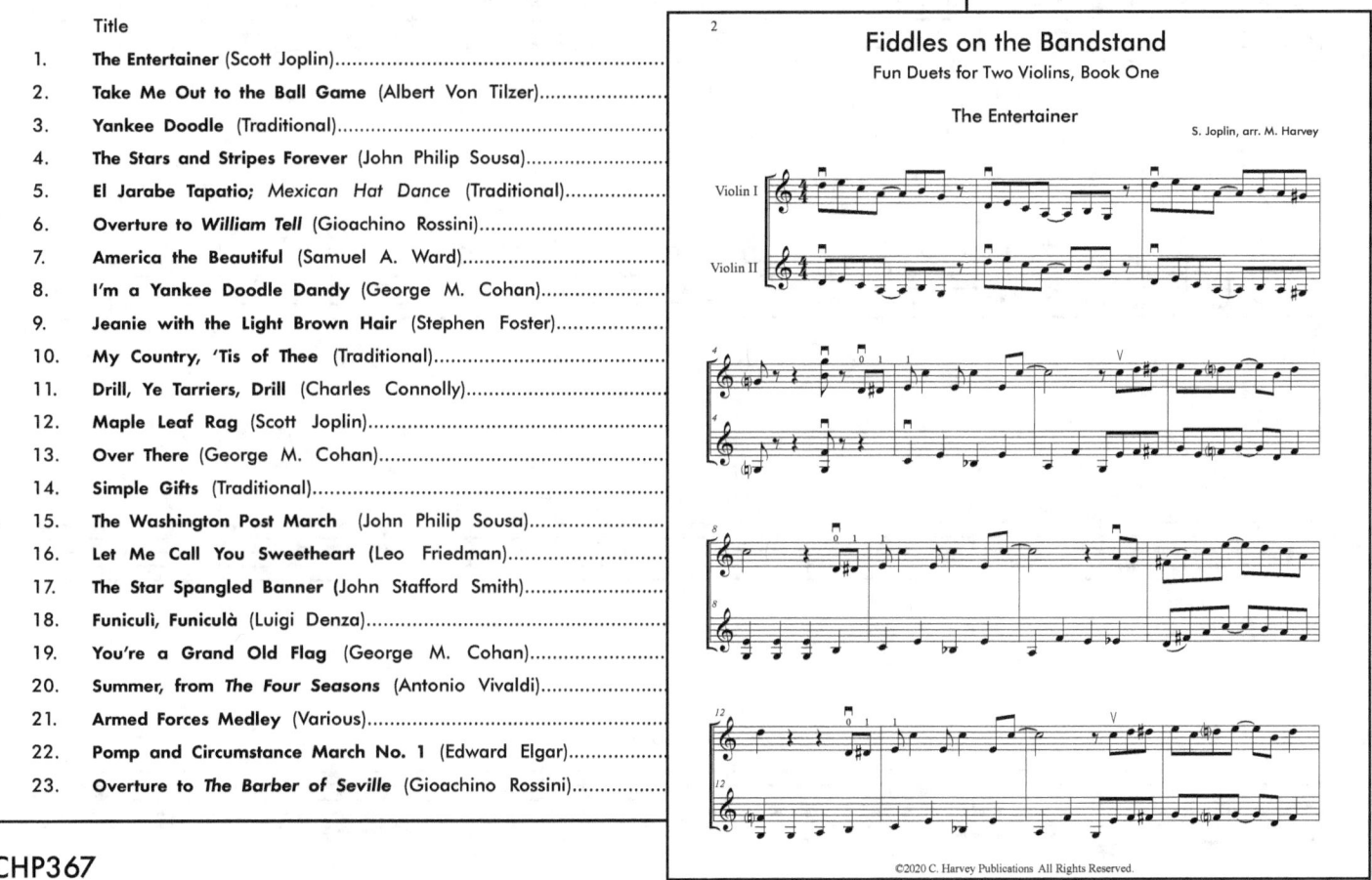

**Fiddles on the Bandstand: Fun Duets for Two Violins
Book One**

all duets arranged by Myanna Harvey

Table of Contents

Title
1. The Entertainer (Scott Joplin).........
2. Take Me Out to the Ball Game (Albert Von Tilzer).........
3. Yankee Doodle (Traditional).........
4. The Stars and Stripes Forever (John Philip Sousa).........
5. El Jarabe Tapatio; Mexican Hat Dance (Traditional).........
6. Overture to William Tell (Gioachino Rossini).........
7. America the Beautiful (Samuel A. Ward).........
8. I'm a Yankee Doodle Dandy (George M. Cohan).........
9. Jeanie with the Light Brown Hair (Stephen Foster).........
10. My Country, 'Tis of Thee (Traditional).........
11. Drill, Ye Tarriers, Drill (Charles Connolly).........
12. Maple Leaf Rag (Scott Joplin).........
13. Over There (George M. Cohan).........
14. Simple Gifts (Traditional).........
15. The Washington Post March (John Philip Sousa).........
16. Let Me Call You Sweetheart (Leo Friedman).........
17. The Star Spangled Banner (John Stafford Smith).........
18. Funiculì, Funiculà (Luigi Denza).........
19. You're a Grand Old Flag (George M. Cohan).........
20. Summer, from The Four Seasons (Antonio Vivaldi).........
21. Armed Forces Medley (Various).........
22. Pomp and Circumstance March No. 1 (Edward Elgar).........
23. Overture to The Barber of Seville (Gioachino Rossini).........

CHP367
$9.95   www.charveypublications.com

Take a journey to a simpler time when lawn chairs and blankets would be out under the stars and music would waft out from under the eaves of the wooden bandstand.

These are the tunes that got our feet moving, made us smile, and brought us together. Now, with these violin duets, you can bring the toe-tapping, exuberant joy to others and remind us all that through highs and lows, music can be something we share to keep our spirits up and build community.

From Scott Joplin to John Philip Sousa, these violin duets will invite you up on the bandstand, out for a gig, or out on your lawn to play your heart out! Know any violists or cellists? You can pick up a copy of the viola or cello book and play with those instruments as well; the violin book is fully compatible with the viola and cello books.

This violin book is mostly in first position, with occasional basic third position.

available from **www.charveypublications.com**: CHP257

G Major Shifting for the Violin

1

Cassia Harvey

©2014 C. Harvey Publications All Rights Reserved.

www.ingramcontent.com/pod-product-compliance
Lightning Source LLC
Chambersburg PA
CBHW051428070526
44584CB00023B/3625